MERIDIAN MIDDLE SCHOOL
2195 Brandywyn Lane
Buffalo Grove, IL 60089

Exercise

for *Weight*

Management

consultant:

Debra Wein, MS, RD

President and Cofounder

www.sensiblenutrition.com

LifeMatters

an imprint of Capstone Press

Mankato, Minnesota

by
Gus
Gedatus

LifeMatters Books are published by Capstone Press
PO Box 669 • 151 Good Counsel Drive • Mankato, Minnesota 56002
http://www.capstone-press.com

SPECIAL ADVISORY AND DISCLAIMER: The information within this book addresses fitness and sports activities that carry significant safety risks, including the risk of serious personal injury. Because this book is general in nature, we recommend that the reader seek qualified professional instruction and advice. We also recommend the use of quality protective equipment when participating in fitness and sports activities. The publisher, its consultants, and the author take no responsibility for the use of any of the materials or methods described in this book nor for the products thereof.

Printed in the United States of America

Library of Congress Cataloging-in-Publication Data
Gedatus, Gustav Mark.
      Exercise for weight management / by Gus Gedatus.
           p.   cm. — (Nutrition and fitness)
      Includes bibliographical references and index.
      ISBN 0-7368-0706-3
      1. Physical fitness—Juvenile literature. 2. Nutrition—Juvenile literature. 3. Weight loss—Juvenile literature. 4. Exercise—Juvenile literature. 5. Body image—Juvenile literature.
      [1. Exercise. 2. Weight control. 3. Physical fitness.] I. Title. II. Series.
      RA781 .G43 2001
      613.7—dc21   00-034899
                                         CIP

Summary: Explains how exercise fits into weight management and discusses exercise activities availab aspects of a safe workout, and creation of a fitness program and goals.

Staff Credits
Rebecca Aldridge, editor; Adam Lazar, designer and illustrator; Kim Danger, photo researcher

Photo Credits
Cover: Stock Market Photo/©Michal Heron
©Artville/Clair Alaska, 17, 59
©DigitalVision/Ronnie Eshel, 37
©Earthstar Stock Inc., 14
FPG International/©Elizabeth Simpson, 13
Index Stock Photos/©Ted Dayton, 19; ©PUSH, 40
©Stockbyte, 27, 38
Unicorn Stock Photos/©Maggie Finefrock, 7; ©Dick Young, 8; ©Aneal S. Vohra, 21; ©Martin R. Jones, 24, 28; ©Rod Furgason, 34; ©Alon Reininger, 56
Uniphoto/©Llewellyn, 45; ©Andy Anderson, 47; ©Allan Laidman, 49; ©Caroline Wood, 55

Table of Contents

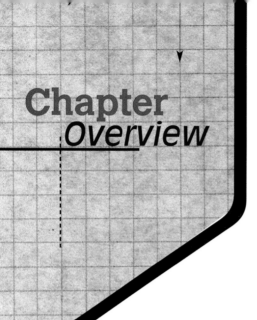

Chapter *Overview*

- Healthy people don't have too much fat on their body. Their heart, lungs, and other body organs all work well.

- Body mass index helps to determine healthy weight. But it's best for teens to see a doctor to determine their healthy weight range.

- A good diet and plenty of sleep are important for healthy living.

- Goal setting and persistence are essential to a program of exercise and weight management.

Chapter 1

Being Fit Means Being Healthy

When you hear the word *healthy*, what comes to mind? Someone who isn't sick? Someone who has no germs? What about someone who weighs too much or too little—is that person healthy?

Many health professionals believe that a truly healthy person has the right amount of muscle without too much fat. Because this person is fit, his or her heart, lungs, and other organs function at their peak. The person has normal blood pressure and a low blood cholesterol count. Cholesterol is a waxy substance made by animals. Too much cholesterol can clog the blood vessels. Eventually, this can lead to heart attack or stroke. Attaining the right amount of muscle compared to body fat is achieved through a regular exercise plan and a healthy diet.

The human body has more than 650 different muscles.

The Right Weight for You

People have different ideas about their own best weight. In many cases, your idea about weight may be a matter of how you feel. Do you feel like you are overweight? Do you find that the simplest physical activities seem like a lot of work? Do you easily run out of breath?

You may have seen charts that list the correct weight for people, based on their height. Unfortunately, these charts don't take into consideration the differences in people's bones and muscle structure. Muscle weighs more than fat does. A muscular person looking at such a chart may find that he or she is classified as overweight.

Some people use body mass index (BMI) to determine the fat-to-muscle ratio in their body. BMI is found by comparing height to weight. Like the weight charts, body mass index categories may not be accurate for everyone. It's a good idea to see a doctor if you are concerned about your weight. A doctor can help to determine what weight range is healthy for your body.

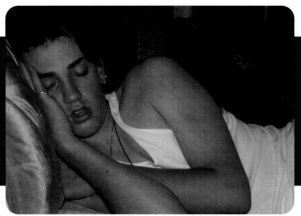

Physical fitness includes getting enough sleep so that you feel well rested when you wake. The right amount of deep sleep helps your body replenish its energy.

Diet and Sleep

To be physically fit, it's important to have a healthy, balanced diet and to get enough sleep. The body requires the vitamins and nutrients, or healthy substances, in different types of foods to work its best. Your body systems work more efficiently if you drink plenty of liquids every day, particularly when you exercise.

The body needs sleep to replenish its energy. A direct relationship exists between exercise and your ability to sleep. When you exercise, you develop more energy for everything. Tasks that used to seem like a lot of work may now be no big deal. Most people feel tired by the end of the day. However, studies have shown that people who exercise sleep more soundly than those who don't exercise. That means people who exercise get stronger health benefits from their sleep time.

Exercise helps you get in shape for sports and simple, everyday activities.

No Bulky Giant

When you think of being fit, you may have some unusual pictures in your mind. Being fit and getting in shape doesn't necessarily mean building bulky muscles to look like a professional body builder. It may mean losing some fat and building more muscle.

Getting in shape means improving how your heart and lungs work. It also means building and strengthening muscles and increasing your flexibility. These things help you have greater freedom to do plenty of enjoyable activities because you won't tire as easily. Being physically fits helps all the systems of your body to function well both now and in your future.

Making and Keeping a Commitment to Yourself

To set up an exercise program for weight control, it helps to do some planning and goal setting. This book may help you with deciding where you want to go with your exercise. It also may help you get a clear idea of the ways you can accomplish your goals. Once you design your exercise program, it's up to you. You're the boss. The success you have comes as a result of your hard work and persistence. It comes from carrying out the commitment you make to yourself.

Your body has approximately 60,000 miles of vessels through which your heart must pump blood. If you are 25 pounds overweight, you have 5,000 more vessels. That means your heart has to work even harder than normal.

Annabel, Age 15

Annabel had never thought of herself as overweight. She was taller than most girls in her class were, and she weighed more, too.

When she was 13, Annabel started running and working out with hand weights. None of her friends were interested in joining her, but she didn't mind. Within a few years, she was doing all sorts of different exercises. She came to really look forward to the wonderful buzz she felt after her workouts.

Annabel is still heavier than most girls her age are. But she feels better, and she likes the way she looks.

Points to Consider

- How do you feel about your present eating habits? Do you think you eat the right foods? Explain.

- Have you noticed any of your own behavior patterns that make you sleep well or not? Explain.

- Have you made commitments to yourself about things other than diet and exercise? Were you successful? What helped or hurt your success?

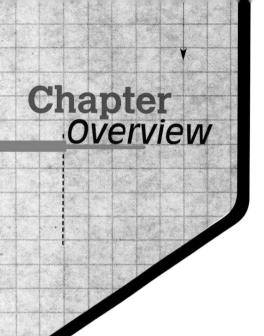

Chapter
Overview

- Metabolism is the body's process of converting food into energy. Muscles work to speed up the metabolism and burn calories faster.

- The best foods to eat include complex carbohydrates, proteins, and fibrous vegetables. High-fat foods should be eaten only in small amounts.

- Many dietary supplements claim to help athletic performance or weight loss. However, these supplements rarely work. They even can be harmful.

- Some changes in eating habits may help people who need to eat less.

- Diets usually do not work for permanent weight loss. To lose weight and keep it off, combine a healthy diet with regular activity and exercise.

Chapter 2

Your Food and Your Body

In thinking about healthy eating choices, how much do you know about good food and not-so-good food? You may know that some foods can add fat. Have you ever thought about food and its relationship to your body's muscles?

How the Body Responds to Food

You may wonder what happens to the food that you eat once it's in your body. How does it give you energy and strength for exercise? What happens that turns food into fat? Understanding some things about metabolism can help you answer those questions. Metabolism is the body's process of converting calories into materials that nourish the body. Calories are the units of energy that your body gets from food. Metabolism enables the body's systems to function.

Everyone's metabolism is a little different. How a person's metabolism works depends upon weight, body makeup, activity level, and age.

An average person's basal metabolic rate (BMR) is about 800 to 900 calories per day. BMR is the amount of energy that you would burn if you did nothing but sleep for 24 hours. This does not include calories burned during digestion, daily activities, or exercise.

Muscles Working for You

You also may wonder why it's important to build muscle. Added muscle mass certainly makes you stronger, but that's not all. Muscles help the body to burn off calories merely by existing. The more muscles you have, the more your metabolism increases, or speeds up. As it increases, your body burns calories faster.

Fat, unlike muscle, simply collects in the body. It doesn't work for you. As your body accumulates more fat, your metabolism slows down. So, the more fat you have, the more fat you are likely to get. However, too little fat can cause health problems as well.

Food energy, particularly in carbohydrates such as bread, rice, and potatoes enters your body as glucose. This is a kind of sugar. Some glucose from carbohydrates is stored as fat. However, a good deal is stored in muscles as glycogen. When you exercise, muscles release their supply of glycogen, which allows your body to use the fat it has stored. As the fuel is used, the fat decreases.

Well-trained muscles more readily store glycogen than muscles that are out of shape. Less-trained muscles use less glycogen during exercise. That's why trained athletes can endure long, hard periods of exercise without getting muscle fatigue. It's possible for you, too. With the proper diet and exercise, you can double the amount of glycogen in your muscles.

The Food Guide Pyramid shows which foods you need to eat more than others.

The Right Foods for Health

The U.S. Department of Agriculture (USDA) developed the Food Guide Pyramid to illustrate a healthy daily eating plan. Similarly, the Canadian government has created a food rainbow called the Canadian Food Guide to Healthy Eating.

The levels of the food pyramid show how many servings people need daily from each food group. These servings are a bit different for teens than for most adults. The lower numbers that follow are recommended for teen girls. The higher numbers are recommended for teen boys.

The bottom level is the bread, cereal, rice, and pasta group. Teens are recommended to get 9 to 11 daily servings from this group. The second level shows that four to five servings of vegetables are needed daily. It also shows that three to four servings of fruits are needed daily. The third level shows both the dairy products and the meat, fish, eggs, beans, and nuts groups. The pyramid recommends three daily servings of dairy products. It suggests two to three servings of meat, fish, eggs, beans, and nuts. The top level includes fat, oils, and sweets, which should be eaten only occasionally.

The darker green the vegetable, the more nutrients it contains.

Serving sizes might be smaller than people think. The following chart gives some examples of food serving sizes.

One-Serving Sizes

Breads/grains: 1 slice of bread, 1 ounce (30 grams) cereal, ½ cup (115 grams) pasta, or ¼ bagel

Vegetables: ½ cup (115 grams) cooked vegetables, 1 cup (225 grams) leafy greens, or ¾ cup (180 milliliters) juice

Fruits: 1 medium piece of fruit, ¾ cup (180 milliliters) juice, or ½ cup (115 grams) canned fruit

Milk foods: 1 cup (240 milliliters) low-fat or nonfat milk, 1 cup (225 grams) yogurt, or 1½ ounces (45 grams) cheese

Meats and meat substitutes: 2 to 3 ounces (60 to 90 grams) lean meat, 2 tablespoons (30 grams) peanut butter, 1 egg, ½ cup (115 grams) beans, or ⅓ cup (150 grams) tofu

Pregnant women, long-distance runners, and people who are healing from broken bones need extra protein.

In thinking about choosing a healthy diet, you can break down the most important foods into three groups:

- **Complex carbohydrates:** These supply the basic energy for your body. They produce glucose for every cell. Complex carbohydrates are the most efficiently burned fuel for your body. They increase your metabolism. Complex carbohydrates include food from the bottom level of the pyramid, as well as potatoes, corn, and beans.

- **Proteins:** Proteins repair injured muscle fiber and help build new muscle. The human body needs about 40 to 56 grams or protein each day to remain in good shape. Meat and dairy foods have the highest amounts of protein. Unfortunately, these two foods are animal proteins that contain high amounts of fat. Some choices of meat and dairy proteins are healthier than others are. White meat chicken, turkey breast, white fish, egg whites, and lean cuts of red meat are good choices. Nonfat milk is a healthy choice, too. Health experts often recommend getting some animal protein as well as protein from beans, rice, whole wheat, and nuts.

- **Fibrous vegetables:** These vegetables contain important vitamins. They also require more energy to digest, so they increase the rate at which calories are burned. Green vegetables and most other vegetables, except for potatoes and corn, are fibrous.

High-Fat Foods

Some foods should be eaten only in small amounts if you want to control your weight. You may decide to eliminate these foods altogether. Think about the foods on this list and in your diet.

- Oils in red meats, butter, and salad dressings; vegetable oils; and foods cooked in oils

- All forms of sugar

- Processed foods such as cold cuts, crackers, chips, and cookies

- Dairy products, except low-fat and nonfat varieties such as skim milk

- Avocados, olives, nuts, and seeds

Supplements

Dietary supplements may come as pills, capsules, liquids, or powders. They may contain vitamins, minerals, amino acids, herbs, or plants. Amino acids build protein. Some people take a supplement because they think it can make them perform better as an athlete. They may take one to help build muscle mass. Some people take supplements that they believe will help them lose weight. Many dietary supplements promise great benefits. Most aren't effective, and some even can be harmful, especially to teens.

Making just a few changes can improve your eating habits, which may help you to eat less.

The Right Eating Habits

People who have weight control concerns often have eating habits in common. They may heap food on their plate. Some may eat too quickly. Many health experts agree that certain habits can contribute to better eating. You can do a few basic things to improve your eating and perhaps eat less.

- **Eat at least five times a day.** This includes two or three reasonable-sized meals and some healthy snacks in between. Try not to let more than four hours pass without eating. If you starve yourself, you lose energy. Then, you may eat too much at the next meal. By eating a little food more often, you help your body. It can better process the food and is less likely to make as much fat.

- **After you take a bite of food, put the utensil down until you have swallowed the bite.** This may take practice, but it can help you eat slower, allowing you to digest your food better.

- **Take a break for three to five minutes during your meal.** Think about whether you're beginning to feel full. Drink some water. Take a few deep breaths.

- **During meals, serve your food in two courses.** Have a low-fat salad and then wait a few minutes before having your main course.

- **When you eat, try to use all of your senses to enjoy the food.** It may slow you down and make your food seem tastier.

"My mom has gone on about 10 weird diets that I can remember. Each time she lost quite a bit of weight, but within a few months she weighed the same as before she started."—Lisa, age 17

- **Before you start eating, set a limit on the amount you will eat.** Stick to your limit.

- **Don't be afraid to leave food on your plate.** If your parents like you to finish everything on your plate, try asking for smaller servings.

- **Don't deny yourself food when you really are hungry.** Have a healthy snack such as raw vegetables.

- **Drink eight 8-ounce (240-milliliter) glasses of water each day.** This helps to keep your body hydrated. That means your body gets enough water to work well. Drinking water also may decrease your feelings of hunger.

Diets Do Not Produce Miracles

In the previous chapter, you read about the importance of a good diet to health and fitness. To have a good diet does not mean to *be* on a diet.

When people go on a diet, they usually adopt a specific eating pattern. They believe this eating pattern will help them to lose weight. They may think that eating certain foods made them put on weight. They may assume that not eating those foods or eating other foods can make the weight go away.

For many years, various companies have offered "miracle diets" that promise great weight loss. Some of these fad diets suggest eating large amounts of protein, while others call for carefully combining certain foods. Still other diets recommend eating large amounts of one food such as grapefruit, cabbage, juice, or broth.

Not drinking enough water can lead to dehydration. This can cause a person to feel tired and lack energy.

High-protein diets usually recommend consuming few or no carbohydrates. Without its regular carbohydrate fuel, the body tends to burn stores of fatty acids. This releases chemicals into the blood. These chemicals can cause headaches, dizziness, and nausea, or feeling the need to throw up, among other things. The extra protein in foods such as meat, cheese, and nuts usually means lots of fat and cholesterol. These substances can contribute to heart disease. Also, many doctors believe that too much protein can harm the kidneys.

Other fad diets, whether focusing on liquids, grapefruit, or cabbage, prevent the body from getting important nutrients. Many fad diets cause stomach problems and a general lack of energy. These diets have one thing in common. They slow down the body's metabolism so it ends up burning less fat.

One particularly dangerous diet suggests that the dieter eat fewer than 1,200 calories per day. This is sometimes called a crash diet. In most people under 60 years of age, the body treats such low calorie intake as starvation. The body's metabolic rate changes a lot. This can cause serious tiredness and lack of energy. The body may retain water and be unable to tolerate cold temperatures. For teens, having too few calories interferes with growth. Crash diets rarely work. More than half of the people who lose weight on them end up gaining back more than they lost.

In many cases, dieters wait for those "miracles" to happen. They may feel disappointment if they fail to lose weight or if they regain weight after losing it. This may lower the person's self-image and raise his or her frustration even more. The simple fact is that a change in eating habits alone cannot take off weight permanently. That's because it does nothing to speed up metabolism. Healthy eating must be combined with an exercise program to manage weight effectively.

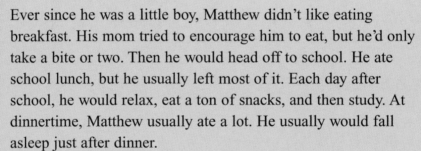

Matthew, Age 14

Ever since he was a little boy, Matthew didn't like eating breakfast. His mom tried to encourage him to eat, but he'd only take a bite or two. Then he would head off to school. He ate school lunch, but he usually left most of it. Each day after school, he would relax, eat a ton of snacks, and then study. At dinnertime, Matthew usually ate a lot. He usually would fall asleep just after dinner.

One day, Matthew decided he wanted to feel better. He started eating cereal with skim milk or toast with peanut butter for breakfast. He made his own lunch of good foods that he liked. After school, he ate fruit and pretzels instead of cookies and corn chips. Now after supper, Matthew has enough energy to go shoot hoops with friends.

Now that Matthew eats breakfast and has healthy snacks throughout the day, he has more energy.

Points to Consider

- Do you think you have a high or low metabolism? Explain.

- In your opinion, what is the best reason for building muscle?

- What about your diet could you change to make it healthier?

- How could you alter your eating habits so you consume less food?

- Have you or anyone you've known had any experience with fad diets? What happened?

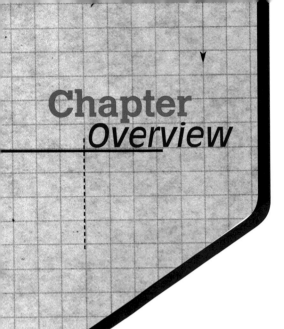

Chapter
Overview

- Aerobic exercise strengthens the heart and lungs and helps to speed up metabolism.

- Many types of aerobic activities are available for you to try.

- Weight training is a valuable anaerobic activity that is particularly useful in combination with aerobic exercise.

- In some cases, a workout partner can encourage you to continue an exercise program.

Chapter 3

Walk, Run, Roll, Glide, Swing, Stroke, or Lift

Ruth, Age 13

Almost every day after school, Ruth and her mom watched a talk show on television. Like the host of the show, Ruth really liked to eat—especially junk food. She didn't care much for exercise. Ruth decided that she was tired of being overweight. It made her feel bad about herself. Ruth and her mom had read about the talk show host's weight loss and exercise program. Ruth and her mom felt that if the host could do it, they could, too.

Ruth and her mom worked on a sensible eating plan. It was really hard to follow at first. They also started working out together. After a while, eating healthy foods seemed natural to both of them. And instead of watching the talk show after school, they would go for a walk together and talk.

Jumping rope burns 200 calories in 20 minutes.

Most people like to have choices. When it comes to exercises for building fitness and managing weight, you have lots of choices. Today, you may have one favorite. Next week, you may have another. After a month or two, you may find that your exercise program has all kinds of variety.

All Kinds of Aerobic Exercises

Fitness experts agree that a good exercise program includes aerobic activities. These exercises use oxygen and are done over and over, so the muscles repeatedly get fresh oxygen. Aerobic exercises speed up your heart rate and breathing. Therefore, they strengthen the heart and lungs.

Aerobic exercises that are done properly raise the metabolism, stimulating the body's fat-burning process. As you become more aerobically fit, you can exercise at higher intensity levels. This means you can burn a larger amount of fat more quickly. The following chart lists popular aerobic exercises and how many calories they burn during a 20-minute workout.

Many fitness experts believe that it's a good idea to determine your pace. This is the number of minutes it takes you to run, walk, or jog one mile or kilometer regularly. Pace may be found by doing one mile or kilometer several days, then figuring an average of these days.

Aerobic Exercises and Calories Burned in 20 Minutes

Walking	110	Swimming	210
Bicycle riding	140	Jogging/running	220
Race walking	160	Cross-country skiing	. . .220
Aerobic dancing	200	Stair stepping	260
Rope jumping	200		

Both brisk walking and jogging are good aerobic exercise. They don't require any special equipment. You can do them most anywhere. Walking doesn't put stress on muscles and joints. On the other hand, jogging does place a lot of stress on joints and ligaments. These are the tough bands of tissue that connect bones. Jogging, however, is considered to provide greater aerobic benefits than walking.

Stair stepping, whether using a stair climber machine or climbing actual steps, puts little stress on your body. It's also easy to learn. Stair stepping uses fewer muscles than jogging or walking but is still good aerobic exercise. Rope jumping is much more vigorous exercise that uses many muscles. It's also something you can easily do at home.

At a Glance

Stretching to increase flexibility is an important part of an exercise program. Dancing and yoga are examples of activities that stretch the muscles.

Cycling, whether riding outside or pedaling inside on a stationary, or still, bike, works mostly the lower body. Rowing is a good activity because it puts little stress on joints and ligaments. It conditions both the upper and lower body. Cross-country skiing is highly aerobic, giving both your arms and legs a hard workout. Swimming is a moderately effective aerobic activity. Usually, the water doesn't let the body heat up enough to affect metabolism. For many people, aerobic classes are a fun way to exercise. The effectiveness of an aerobics class lies in the hands of the leader, who develops movement routines.

It's a good idea to cross-train with aerobic activities. For instance, you may want to alternate walking with biking or swimming, or tennis with in-line skating. Cross-training can help you gain more balanced fitness and help prevent injury.

Weight Training

Combining weight training with a program of aerobic exercise is a good idea. Weight training is anaerobic exercise. This exercise is so demanding that it cannot be supported by the body's oxygen supply. Therefore, you feel stressed quickly. The more fit you are, the longer it takes for your body to run out of oxygen.

Weight training elevates your heart rate, but it doesn't use a lot of oxygen. Therefore, it doesn't directly benefit your heart or lungs. It doesn't speed up your metabolism, either. However, weight training helps to build muscles. This increases your calorie-burning process. Muscles are active tissues with high energy requirements. Muscles are responsible for more than 25 percent of your calorie use even when you're asleep.

Weight training builds and tones muscles. This is important because muscle tissue burns more calories at rest than fat does.

If you want to include weight training in your exercise, great! But if you're new to it, start with light weights. Don't try to lift too much in your first weeks. You may hurt yourself or develop aches and pains that may discourage you from keeping at it. Ask a coach or physical education teacher to help you with proper lifts.

You may want to concentrate on specific muscles. However, a well-rounded program helps to maintain a balance within your body.

If you are beginning a weight training program, do your aerobics first. They provide a good warm-up for working with the weights.

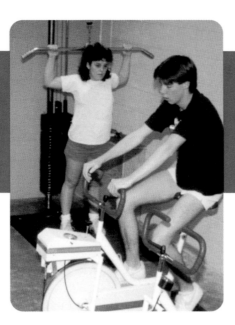

Having someone to work out with can help keep you motivated. It also can make exercise more enjoyable.

As you plan your weight training workout, you will want to think in terms of reps and sets. A rep is a repetition of one type of exercise movement, from start to middle to finish. A set is a number of reps that you plan for a given workout. For example, you might do 10 reps of biceps curls. This move works the upper muscle on the front of your arm. These 10 reps are one set. You might start out with two sets.

By weight training, you not only build muscle but also increase your strength and energy. Over time, weight training can tone your muscles and help improve your posture. Your bones will get stronger, too.

"I didn't really want to spend money on weights, so I just use some empty milk cartons that I fill with sand."—Deyanne, age 14

A Workout Partner

Many people like to exercise with a partner. In some cases, a partner may help you stick to your workout program. He or she usually counts on you to be on schedule and show up for your exercise as planned. A partner can help if you're having a bad day. He or she might be able to get you into some exercise that will improve your mood. Most importantly, many people feel that working out with a friend can make the process a lot more fun. Of course, if working out is fun, you're more likely to stick with it.

If you decide to look for a workout partner, find someone whose workout goals are similar to yours. Find someone with a fitness level close to your own. Be honest about your available time and your obligations. Come to an agreement about schedules and your commitment to one another. Remember that if you want to have a reliable partner, you have to be one, too. Communicate with your partner if you need to make changes in plans. Be supportive of the other person in her or his exercise progress. Treat the person as you want to be treated.

Keep in mind that as you progress, your or your partner's needs or goals may change. If that happens, it may be time to find a different workout partner, and that's okay.

For many people, the more sedentary you become, the more your appetite increases. To be sedentary means to do a lot of sitting.

Donnel, Age 16

Donnel wasn't overweight, but he wanted to make sure he kept his weight down. When he planned a workout program, he asked his friend Charles to be his partner. He thought that would help him stay with it and make it more fun.

For the first few weeks, Donnel and Charles made a great workout team. But after a while, Donnel could tell that he was enjoying the workouts more than Charles was. As the weeks passed, Charles came up with many reasons why he had to skip their workouts. Donnel didn't want Charles's attitude to affect his own desire to work out. He let Charles know that he needed to find a different partner. Donnel and Charles are still good friends. They just aren't workout partners any longer.

Myth: You can sweat off fat.

Fact: You may seem to lose weight immediately if you perspire, or sweat, a lot during a workout. However, that loss is most likely from water that has left the body, not fat.

Myth vs. Fact

Points to Consider

- Which types of aerobic exercise most appeal to you? Why?

- What would be the best combination of different types of aerobic exercises for you?

- Is weight training something you would like to do? Why or why not?

- For you, what would be the advantages of having a workout partner?

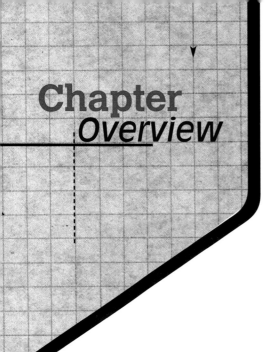

Chapter
Overview

- The progress you make in your exercise program depends upon the frequency, duration, and intensity of your exercise.

- Many fitness experts recommend a combination of aerobics and weight training.

- To be successful with an exercise program, set realistic goals.

- Be determined but patient.

- Keeping a workout journal may be one way to track your progress and motivate yourself.

Chapter 4

Setting Up an Exercise Program

Frequency, Duration, and Intensity

Most of the planning of a program for getting and staying fit involves three considerations: frequency, duration, and intensity.

- **Frequency is how often you exercise.** Most experts recommend three sessions a week for beginners. The goal you're working toward is to do at least three to five 30-minute sessions each week.

- **Duration is how long you exercise.** The duration you start with depends on the particular exercise. It also depends on what sort of shape you are in before you begin.

- **Intensity is how hard you work.** This could be how far you run, how much weight you lift, or how much you raise your heart rate. To most people, a workout that is intense enough goes just beyond what is comfortable.

Cross-country skiing can help you work both lower-body and upper-body muscles.

Many people measure their workout intensity level by using their maximum heart rate. You can check your maximum heart rate by exercising until you're too tired to go on. Then take your pulse. As you exercise and become more fit, your maximum heart rate should increase.

Some people believe that a person's maximum heart rate can be computed by subtracting one's age from 220. For instance, if you are 15 years old, your maximum heart rate may be 205. However, this formula doesn't work for about 30 percent of people. That's because, although they are perfectly healthy, their heart beats faster or slower than average.

A low-intensity workout provides a good beginning. By gradually adding more strenuous activity, your body adapts slowly as it learns to burn more fat calories. As your body becomes more conditioned, you can increase the frequency and duration of your workouts.

You may want to start with easy activities such as brisk walking or riding a stationary bike at a moderate pace. It would be great to do this for about 30 minutes. However, if that's too much, plan on starting at 10 to 15 minutes. Gradually increase the length of time you exercise.

Different Levels, Different Routines

As mentioned earlier, a good exercise regimen, or program, for weight control includes both aerobic activities and weight training. How you design your program is entirely your decision. Let's assume that you include some form of aerobic exercise and some weight training.

Once you choose your primary aerobic exercise, your goal is to do it in a comfortable, continuous rhythm. This gives you the best results. If you have to slow down to do this, then slow down. It's better to work at a constant yet slow pace, rather than a clumsy yet fast one.

You may decide to do more than one type of aerobic activity in your workout. If so, at least one activity should involve the large muscle groups, mostly those in the lower body. Don't forget to start out easy with the type of exercise, as well as the frequency, duration, and intensity. If you try to do too much too soon, you can develop sore muscles and even injuries. If you're concerned about spending more time working the upper part of your body, be patient. As you progress, you can take on other activities such as cross-country skiing or using a rowing machine.

It's essential to start out slowly with a weight training program. Keep your enthusiasm for your workout, but make sure to use good judgment in protecting yourself from injury. You may be able to lift a heavy weight. That doesn't mean you should do lots of reps with it. Start out with a light weight and build upward. Vary your exercise routines to focus on many different muscle groups. Do this from the beginning, even when you're using very light weights. It will get you and your muscle groups into an important growing pattern.

Warm-ups and stretches are important to do before your exercise. These activities are discussed in Chapter 5.

You might get some ideas for a workout program by taking a look at Brenda's early fitness plan. Brenda is 15 years old. This is her first exercise program.

Brenda's Fitness Plan

June

Week 1

Two times a week
- 30 minutes bike riding
- No weights yet

Week 2

Two times a week
- 30 minutes bike riding, 15 minutes dancing

July

Week 1

Three times a week
- 30 minutes swimming, 15 minutes brisk walking
- 25 minutes 4 sets of light weights

Week 2

Three times a week
- 30 minutes swimming, 20 minutes bike riding
- 25 minutes 4 sets of light weights

August

Week 1

Four times a week
- 25 minutes swimming, 15 minutes rowing machine
- 30 minutes 5 sets of light weights

Week 2

Four times a week
- 25 minutes bike riding, 15 minutes rowing machine
- 30 minutes 5 sets of light weights

Dancing is one example of fun aerobic exercise.

Week 3	Week 4
Three times a week	**Three times a week**
• 20 minutes dancing, 20 minutes brisk walking • 20 minutes 3 sets of light weights	• 30 minutes in-line skating, 15 minutes brisk walking • 20 minutes 3 sets of light weights

Week 3	Week 4
Four times a week	**Four times a week**
• 15 minutes stair stepping, 30 minutes aerobics class • 25 minutes 4 sets of light weights	• 15 minutes stair stepping, 30 minutes bike riding • 25 minutes 4 sets of light weights

Week 3	Week 4
Four times a week	**Four times a week**
• 20 minutes aerobics class, 20 minutes brisk walking • 30 minutes 7 sets of light weights	• 20 minutes aerobics class, 20 minutes rowing machine • 30 minutes 7 sets of light weights

When you reach a goal, you might want to reward yourself. If you like music, maybe you'll buy a new CD.

Goals to Take You There

In setting up an exercise program, set goals for different times. What do you hope to accomplish this week? this month? in three months? during the next year? Maybe you can do 15 push-ups in a row now. Your goal might be to do 30 in a row in six weeks. After you set your goals, you try to reach them. However, be flexible with yourself if those goals need to be changed.

For some people, having a role model is helpful. You may know of someone who set out to become more physically fit and accomplished great things. Let yourself be motivated by that person's success.

When you reach a goal, reward yourself. For example, you could plan to buy a CD or a new outfit or just spend an evening with friends. Acknowledge the fact that you set out to reach a goal and succeeded. Keep a record of your progress in a workout journal. This is discussed later in this chapter.

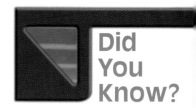

Determination With Patience

When people start an exercise program, they often have lots of enthusiasm for it. However, in many cases, these feelings lapse. For different reasons, the pattern of exercise may decrease until the person doesn't do it at all. You can do a few things to prevent this from happening.

- **Start out with manageable exercises that don't cause discomfort.** You may find lots of reasons not to exercise if it makes you tired and sore. On the other hand, exercise should be challenging enough to keep it interesting.

- **As mentioned, a workout partner may help you stick to your exercise program.**

- **Use your exercise time wisely.** You have many things going on in your life, so respect your time and energy limits. You don't want to burn out before you have accomplished great things.

- **Make your exercise surroundings comfortable.** Do whatever you can to make your workout experience more enjoyable. Maybe listen to some music.

- **Think about your goals and how much it means to you to improve your life and health.**

Recording your workouts in a journal can help you get an idea of what works well for you and what doesn't.

Keeping a Workout Journal

Keeping a workout journal can be a good idea. This may help you keep on track with where you're going and where you have yet to go. When you consider adding variety to your workout, a journal may help you to create a balance. In reviewing your journal, you may see patterns of things that helped you stick to your program. You may identify some obstacles that you can eliminate. This may make your workout more productive or more enjoyable.

Some people carry their journal with them when they work out. They start out each session with a list of activities. Then they check off these activities as they're completed. Doing this may be one way to keep a regular pattern during your exercise program.

Some people make their journal more than just a record of their workouts. They may record how much water they drink, how much sleep they get, or which foods they eat. This information helps them to live an even healthier life.

"Work out first thing in the morning. Then you don't have so many other things that could get in the way. When I exercise first thing in the morning, I feel better all day long."—C. J., age 15

Diego, Age 16

Diego never does anything halfway. He keeps a detailed journal. It includes not only his workout plan but also a record of all the food he eats.

When he looks back at his journal each week, Diego learns a lot. Now, he knows that he works best when there's music playing. He's more into his workouts in the morning than in the evening. Diego has learned something about his eating, too. When he eats a few pieces of fruit during the day, he isn't likely to pig out after school.

Points to Consider

- In planning your workout program, what would you want to consider?

- Once you set goals, would you be able to alter them easily if they weren't the right ones? Why or why not?

- What challenges would you face in following through with an exercise program?

- What would you include in a workout journal? How would this information be useful?

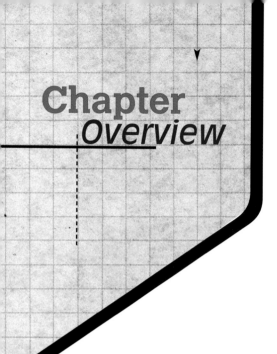

Chapter Overview

- Warm-ups, stretches, and cool-downs are important when exercising.

- During strenuous exercise, it's essential that you keep your body hydrated. Also, special precautions should be taken when you exercise in warm weather.

- Cross-training and avoiding common mistakes can help to make your workout program most effective.

- For some people, exercise can become an unhealthy addiction.

Chapter 5

The Right Approach

Warm-Ups, Stretches, and Cool-Downs

Before you begin your exercising, it's important to warm up. A warm-up often is a slow, easy version of the planned activity. Some people do easy jogging, rope jumping, or biking. The length of time for a warm-up should relate to how hard you plan to exercise. The type of warm-up and its intensity also should relate to the level of your workout.

As your muscles warm up gradually, it's easier for oxygen to leave the blood and pass into the muscles. If you begin hard exercise without warming up first, your muscles are starved for oxygen during the first few minutes. You may run out of breath easily if this happens. In some people, the lack of oxygen can cause painful muscle cramps. This also may happen because cold muscles aren't very elastic. Warmed muscles are less likely to be injured by sudden or extreme movement.

Caffeine is a diuretic. That means it promotes water loss from the body. If you drink soda full of caffeine before you exercise, it could contribute to dehydration. If you're unsure about whether what you're drinking contains caffeine, check the container. There may be more than you expect. For instance, 8 ounces (240 milliliters) of cola has approximately 40 milligrams of caffeine. Some soft drinks have as much as 54 milligrams of caffeine.

When you are warmed up, your nervous system operates more effectively. If you're involved in activity that requires intricate movements, this is especially important. A warmed-up nervous system can help you to perform at your best. Not to mention, warmed-up muscles burn fat more effectively than cold muscles do.

After you warm up, do some stretching. When you stretch, hold each stretch for a few seconds. Don't bounce during your stretch. Rest. Then, repeat the stretch for a few seconds. Devote two minutes or more to each muscle group you're stretching. Stretch for 5 to 10 minutes before you exercise and for the same amount of time afterward.

Stretching prepares your muscles for the exercise activity to come. It helps prevent muscles from getting injured.

At the end of your exercise period, do some varied, easy movements to cool down. This activity lets your heart rate decrease gradually. For example, you could walk at an easy pace. Cooling down also helps your normal blood flow return. Without a cool-down, your blood may pool in the lower part of your body. As your brain receives less blood than normal, you may feel dizziness and fatigue.

Keeping Your Body Hydrated

The human body sweats to remain cool. Body temperature must be kept under control, or body organs would be destroyed. When we perspire, water leaves the blood. Then the blood becomes thicker and movement becomes more work. The lungs don't pick up as much oxygen when blood is thickened because movement for breathing is reduced, too. That is why it's important to replenish the body's water supply by stopping to take drinks during exercise.

Fast Fact

During exercise, the body produces 10 to 15 times as much heat as when you're at rest. When you exercise hard, you produce enough heat to evaporate 2 quarts (1.9 liters) of water in one hour.

It's a good idea to drink at least 1 cup (240 milliliters) of water about 30 minutes before exercising. Every 15 to 20 minutes during exercise, drink at least another 3 to 6 ounces (89 to 178 milliliters). Don't wait until you're thirsty. Instead, follow a regular schedule. If you wait until you are thirsty, you're already becoming dehydrated. Drink cool fluids rather than warm or ice-cold beverages. Fluids at 40 to 50 degrees Fahrenheit (F) (4.4 to 10 degrees Celsius [C]) pass through the stomach and into the bloodstream more quickly. When you finish your exercise, drink some more water.

When the Weather Is Warm

On warm, sunny days you may be eager to exercise in the outdoors. That's terrific! However, keep in mind a few things to remain safe and healthy.

If you can, exercise in the morning or evening when it's a bit cooler. Wear loose-fitting clothing made of fabrics that let heat escape. It's helpful to carry a water bottle. The regular sips of water help control your body temperature.

It's important to drink water before, during, and after exercise.

When the air temperature is over 90 degrees F (32 degrees C), don't work out too hard. This is especially important if both the humidity and the temperature are high. During normal workouts, your perspiration evaporates to keep you cool. In hot, humid weather, this evaporation doesn't happen as quickly. You could become overheated. In warm weather, don't work out too hard in a heated pool. Even though you're in water, your body still can heat up too much. Also, drink a lot of water, even during swim workouts.

If you start to feel dizzy or if you get a sudden stomachache or headache, stop exercising. Rest in a cooler, shady place until you feel better. Drink some water.

"Whenever I do some new kind of exercise, I may end up with some different stiffness or pain the next day. Instead of laying off that exercise, I do it again the very next day. But I do it at an easier pace. It seems like once my body is used to the exercise, the stiffness goes away."
—Kenyon, age 14

Common Mistakes

People sometimes make mistakes that cause their workouts to be less effective. Other mistakes may cause serious injuries. The American Council on Exercise (ACE) interviewed 3,000 fitness instructors. It got this list of recommendations from them for avoiding common workout mistakes.

- Always warm up before aerobic activity. Don't rush those warm-ups.

- Stretch your muscles before and after your exercise. Stretch any muscles that were used a lot during exercise.

- Cool down after a workout.

- If you are weight training, don't lift too much weight too quickly. Work up to heavier weights gradually to avoid potentially serious injuries.

Tennis can be good cross-training with bicycling or in-line skating. That's because it works upper-body muscles, while biking or skating works lower-body muscles.

- Use controlled, slow movements when weight training. Sudden, jerking movements can cause injuries, especially to your back.

- Avoid short, very intense workouts. It's more effective for the average person to do longer periods of moderate workouts.

- Make sure to get your heart rate elevated when you work out. Otherwise, you aren't getting as many health benefits.

- Drink at least eight glasses of water a day, especially on workout days.

Cross-Training

As mentioned earlier, you may well get into a pattern of exercise that includes combining your favorite activities. For instance, maybe you love bicycling and in-line skating. However, while such sports benefit your whole body, they're of the greatest benefit to your lower-body muscles. You might play tennis to get a more diverse workout than you get from bicycling.

Jogging, for instance, is an effective aerobic exercise. For some people, too much jogging can cause problems. This is because jogging is a high-impact activity that places stress on joints and tendons. Jogging is a perfect example of something you would want to combine with other activities. Jog one day. In-line skate or bicycle the next. And you know what? As you cross-train with different types of activities, you're much less likely to become bored with your exercise program.

Exercise Addiction

Exercise can become an addiction for some people. Signs of exercise addiction can include:

- Dropping scheduled plans to exercise instead

- Feeling depressed or extremely guilty when unable to work out

- Spending less and less time with friends and family to exercise

Addiction to exercise is harmful because it can cause serious injury from muscle strain. It also can cause arthritis, which is the painful swelling of joints. Too much exercise can damage the immune system. This body system keeps a person from getting sick. Exercise addiction can cause poor concentration, too. Sometimes exercise addiction is combined with an eating disorder.

People addicted to exercise need to talk with someone. A counselor may be able to help. This person can help people who have exercise addiction figure out what makes them want to work out so much. A counselor can help them get back to a daily activity schedule that's healthy.

Points to Consider

- Describe a warm-up routine that you would do.

- How would you cope with exercising in warm weather?

- What cross-training would you want to do? Why?

- What do you think would be an example of too much exercise?

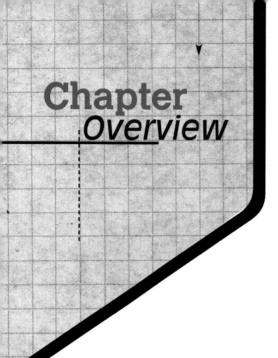

Chapter *Overview*

- Added activity and several daily habits can give you a fitness boost.

- Regular physical exercise can help you reduce stress. With less stress, you may have more energy for activities that are fun.

- Regular exercise and weight management can help prevent many types of disease. People whose weight is under control are less likely to become seriously ill.

- You may someday be a fitness model for someone else.

Chapter 6

A Fitness Pattern for Life

Add Activity to Your Day

Some guidelines suggest 60 minutes of moderate activity most every day for children and teens. These same guidelines suggest 30 minutes of this activity per day for adults. So what exactly is moderate activity? It's any activity that uses about the same amount of energy as walking 2 miles (3.2 kilometers) in 30 minutes. You may think, "Wow, 60 minutes of exercise, that's a lot." But this is overall activity. You don't necessarily have to jog for an hour straight. You can break this time up into sections—10 minutes here, 10 minutes there.

Also, this activity doesn't have to include typical exercise. Raking leaves, mowing the lawn, and cleaning your room are all physical activities that count! And if you can't do 60 minutes a day, don't panic. Remember that some exercise is always better than no exercise at all.

Advice From Teens

"Whatever you do, don't get into a pattern of weighing yourself. This could discourage you if your weight goes up and down like mine did. I was ready to give up after only a month."
—Celia, age 15

Good Everyday Habits

You can do some things every day to increase your activity level and control your eating. Once you get into these habits, they're usually no big deal. Over time, they can add to your successful weight management.

- Whenever you walk, get in the habit of taking bigger steps and walking more quickly.

- If you have the choice of taking an elevator or stairs, take the stairs whenever possible.

- Don't sit still for more than an hour at a time. Get up and move around for any reason—even just pacing.

- If you can walk somewhere or ride a bike instead of riding in a bus or car, do it.

- Get involved in a hobby or two that include enjoyable exercise. Gardening and dancing are two examples you might consider.

Instead of just lying outside on a sunny day, do something fun, such as kayaking.

- If you're outside enjoying the sun, don't just lie there. Swim, row a boat, paddle a canoe, or water-ski.

- Take a brief walk after each meal. A walk can help speed up your metabolism and aid digestion.

- Don't eat unless you are sitting down and the food is on a plate.

- Don't eat while talking on the telephone.

- Don't become too involved with other activities while you're eating. For example, if you watch TV while you eat, you may not pay attention to how much you're eating. You may end up eating too much.

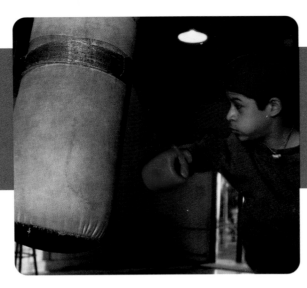

Exercise can help you to handle stress.

Francis, Age 17

Francis had been in trouble many times since he was young. Like his father, he had a strong temper. If someone made fun of him, it usually led to a fight. Sometimes he won, sometimes he didn't.

When he was in the eighth grade, Francis started jogging and working out with weights. He even got a punching bag. After each half-hour session of pounding that bag, Francis felt a little bit stronger. But even better—he no longer seemed so angry. Now, when someone or something upsets Francis, he works it out of his system by exercising.

Exercise—A Sensible Stress Reliever

Have you ever said, "I got so upset. I thought I would explode"? What happens when you feel that way? Do you do or say things that only make matters worse? Do you find that you become exhausted, not from physical activity, but simply from all the stress?

Exercise helps to burn off the body chemicals that build up when you feel stressed. Exercise also produces body chemicals called endorphins that help you to relax and feel good. Therefore, if you get regular exercise and eat right, you can better handle everyday stress. You may find that it's easier to remain positive during your day. Problems will still come up, but they may not seem so impossible.

In reducing the worry of stress, you may be likely to avoid many stress-related illnesses both now and in the future. Also, when you decrease the stress in your life, you keep more energy for things that are fun.

By managing your weight through exercise, you may find that simple daily tasks become easier for you. When someone is overweight, many activities seem like a lot of work because of the added weight. Obviously, if you decrease the strain and fatigue of your daily life, you reduce stress, too.

"By eating less, you actually slow your metabolism down, so the body is burning fewer calories; and dieting does nothing in the way of increasing muscle tone and definition. The only way to achieve optimal fitness, and by that I mean weight loss and increased muscle mass, tone, and definition, is to incorporate cardiovascular [aerobic] exercise into your workout routine."
—Dr. Herman Falsetti, a cardiologist from Irvine, California

Fitness as Protection Against Future Disease

You may have no serious health problems at the present time. Wouldn't it be terrific if you didn't have any ever? You can make that one of your goals.

Researchers have found that weight management and regular physical activity can help you prevent the following health problems:

- Heart disease

- Stroke

- High blood pressure

- Some forms of diabetes (a disease in which there is too much sugar in the blood)

- Gallbladder disease (the gallbladder stores bile, a liquid that helps digest food)

- Back pain

- Osteoporosis (a disease that causes bones to become fragile)

- Arthritis

Exercising to manage your weight can help you stay healthy and happy.

You Can Set a Good Example

You may well set a good example of fitness for others. Maybe you have younger brothers and sisters. Someday, you might even have children of your own. Isn't it possible that you would feel great because some young person saw you as a role model?

Points to Consider

- Which everyday fitness habits could you adopt without any real trouble?

- What things make you feel stressed out? Do you think exercise could help? Why or why not?

- When you've done some hard exercise in the past, how did you feel afterward?

- Do you think exercise can make a person happier? Why or why not?

- Have you ever been a role model for anyone? How do you think it feels to be a role model?

At publication, all resources listed here were accurate and appropriate to the topics covered in this book. Addresses and phone numbers may change. When visiting Internet sites and links, use good judgment. Remember, never give personal information over the Internet.

Internet Sites

American Council on Exercise
www.acefitness.org
Provides information on fitness and exercise for teens and adults

FitTeen.com
www.fitteen.com
Offers a teen-fitness chat room, workout charts, sample routines, and a fitness glossary

Go Ask Alice
www.goaskalice.columbia.edu/index.html
Contains health information for teens, including fitness and nutrition information

Shape Up America!
www.shapeup.org
Has information on safe weight management, healthy eating, and increased activity

Teenage Health Interactive Network (THINK)
http://library.thinkquest.org/29500
Run by teens for teens and covers health, nutrition, and fitness

Useful Addresses

American Dietetic Association (ADA)
216 West Jackson Boulevard
Chicago, IL 60606-6995
1-800-366-1655
www.eatright.org

Health Canada
Childhood and Youth Division
Ninth Floor Jeanne Mance Building
Tunney's Pasture, Mail Stop 1909C2
Ottawa, ON K1A 0K9
CANADA

President's Council on Physical Fitness and
Sports
Hubert H. Humphrey Building, Room 738-H
200 Independence Avenue Southwest
Washington, DC 20201

United States Department of Agriculture
Center for Nutrition Policy and Promotion
1120 20th Street Northwest
Suite 200, North Lobby
Washington, DC 20036

Weight Control Information Network
1 WIN Way
Bethesda, MD 20893-3665
1-800-WIN-8098 (800-946-8098)

For Further Reading

Faigenbaum, Avery D., and Wayne L. Westcott. *Strength and Power for Young Athletes.*
        Champaign, IL: Human Kinetics, 2000.

Fraser, K., and Judy Tatchell. *Fitness and Health.* Tulsa, OK: EDC Publishing, 1999.

Gedatus, Gus. *Bicycling for Fitness.* Mankato, MN: Capstone, 2001.

Gedatus, Gus. *Weight Training.* Mankato, MN: Capstone, 2001.

Green, Tamara. *Exercise Is Fun.* Milwaukee: Gareth Stevens, 1998.

Schwager, Tina. *The Right Moves: A Girl's Guide to Getting Fit and Feeling Good.* Minneapolis:
        Free Spirit, 1998.

Turck, Mary. *Healthy Eating for Weight Management.* Mankato, MN: Capstone, 2001.

Glossary

aerobic (air-OH-bik)—rhythmic, continual, and energetic exercise that strengthens the heart and improves breathing

anaerobic (AN-air-oh-bik)—activity in which the body temporarily depletes its supply of oxygen

calorie (KAL-uh-ree)—a measurement of the amount of energy that a food gives

cardiovascular (kar-dee-oh-VASS-kyuh-lur)—relating to the heart and blood vessels

dehydrated (dee-HYE-dray-tid)—lacking enough water in the body

duration (du-RAY-shuhn)—the period of time during which something lasts

frequency (FREE-kwuhn-see)—the number of times that something happens

glucose (GLOO-kohss)—a natural sugar that gives energy to living things

glycogen (GLYE-kuh-juhn)—the main form in which carbohydrates are stored in tissue, especially muscle tissue

hydrate (HYE-drayt)—to add water to

intensity (in-TEN-suh-tee)—how strong something is

intermediate (in-tur-MEE-dee-it)—between two things or in the middle

metabolism (muh-TAB-uh-liz-uhm)—the process by which the body changes food into energy

regimen (REJ-uh-muhn)—a system or pattern for doing something

sedentary (SEH-duhn-tair-ee)—doing or requiring much sitting

Index

addiction, 50–51

aerobic exercise, 24–26, 27, 35, 37, 48, 50

anaerobic exercise, 26

arthritis, 50, 58

blood pressure, 5, 58

body fat. *See* fat

body mass index (BMI), 6

bones, 6, 28

boredom, 39, 50

bread/grains, 13, 14, 15, 20

breakfast, 20, 21

calories, 11, 12, 19, 24, 25, 26, 27, 34

Canadian Food Guide to Healthy Eating, 13

carbohydrates, 12, 19

    complex, 15

cholesterol, 5, 19

commitment, 8, 29

cool-downs, 43, 45, 48

counselors, 51

crash diets, 19. *See also* dieting

cross-training, 26, 49–50

dairy products, 13, 14, 15, 20

dehydration, 19, 45, 46

determination, 39

diet, 5, 7, 11–21, 40, 41. *See also* serving sizes

    and improving eating habits, 17–18, 23

    and your nutritional needs, 13

dieting, 18–20. *See also* crash diets

    fad, 18, 19

digestion, 12, 17, 55

disease prevention, 58

doctors, 6

duration, 33–34, 35

eating disorders, 50

endorphins, 57

energy, 7, 11, 12, 15, 17, 19, 20, 21, 28, 57

exercise, 5, 20, 46, 47, 56–57, 59. *See also* addiction; cool-downs; cross-training; stretching; warm-ups; weight training

    aerobic, 24–26, 27, 35, 37, 48, 50

    increasing from daily activities, 8, 53, 54–55

    liquid intake during, 7, 45–46, 47

    program, 8, 24, 28–29, 30, 33–41

    workout partners, 23, 28–29, 30, 39

fat, 5, 6, 8, 12, 15, 17, 19, 24, 27, 31, 34, 44

fats, oils, sweets, 13, 16

fiber, 15

flexibility, 8, 26

food. *See* diet

frequency, 33–34, 35

friends, 28, 30, 38

fruits, 13, 14, 18, 19, 20

glycogen, 12

goals, 8, 29, 38, 39

habits,

    activity, 53, 54–55

    eating, 17–18

Index

heart, 5, 8, 9, 19, 24, 26, 58
    rate, 24, 26, 33, 34, 35, 45, 49

injury prevention, 26, 35, 43, 48–49, 50
intensity, 24, 33–34, 35, 49

journals, 38, 40–41

liquids, 7, 44, 45–46. *See also* water
lungs, 5, 8, 24, 26

meat and meat substitutes, 13, 14, 15.
    See also proteins
metabolism, 11, 12, 15, 19, 20, 24, 26, 55, 58
mood changes, 28, 29, 56–57
muscle, 5, 12, 24, 25, 27, 43, 44, 45, 48, 49, 50
    building, 8, 16, 26–28
    strengthening, 8, 28
    structure, 6, 39
myths, 31

nutrients, 7, 19
nutrition, 13

overheating, 45, 47
oxygen, 24, 26, 43, 45

pace, 25
physical activity. *See* exercise
posture, 28
proteins, 15, 16, 18–19. *See also* meat
    and meat substitutes

rewards, 38
role models, 38, 59

self-image, 9, 20, 23
serving sizes, 14, 17
sleep, 7, 26
snacks, 17, 20, 21
starvation, 17, 19
stress, 25, 50, 56–57
stretching, 26, 36, 43, 44, 48
supplements, food, 16

tired, feeling, 8, 19, 45

U.S. Food Guide Pyramid, 13

vegetables, 13, 14, 15, 18, 19
vitamins, 7, 15

walking, 23, 25, 36–37, 45, 53, 54, 55
warm-ups, 27, 36, 43–44, 48
water, 17, 18, 19, 31, 40, 45–46, 47, 49
weather, warm, 46–47
weight, 11
    healthy, 6
    loss, 16, 18–20, 23
    management, 16, 17–18, 30, 54–55, 57, 59
    over-, 6, 9, 12, 23, 57
    regaining, 18, 20
    under-, 12
weight training, 9, 26–28, 29, 35, 36–37, 48–49, 56